Slimy

A true story about the
devastation of bullying.

Written by

Karen Slimick Arnpriester

The Swing Incident

Quickly, a crowd of kids had surrounded me, laughing and pointing, or chanting the numbers with me. A nauseating dread filled me when I realized that I was no longer invisible, but I couldn't back down now; not with everyone watching. Our counting was almost to thirty, the magical number that gave me the right to claim a swing from a child who already had a turn. The boy on the swing in front of me did not slow down, and he grinned as an evil plan developed in his head.

As the clamor of voices yelled out "thirty," the boy leapt off of the swing, bringing up one foot, which slammed into my pelvis. I fell to the ground with an incredible jarring pain. The circle of kids packed in tighter, laughing and cheering for the boy.

I laid there, mortified and unable to hold the throbbing private area, which we all do if you think about it. Somehow it helps. They would not have the satisfaction of seeing me touch myself, not there. I balled up, and struggled not to cry, they could not see me cry. When the bell rang, the taunting mob scattered to their rooms.

Lying there, alone, tears streaming down my face, I tried to sort out what had just happened. I didn't understand why they all hated me; I didn't do anything to them that would make this extreme abuse reasonable. Was being different so terrible? They liked different colors, TV shows, and ice cream flavors. It seemed that more choices and variety was a good thing, except when it came to people. Who said we were all supposed to look alike, sound alike and act alike?

I don't know how long I laid there in my pain and shame. It felt like an eternity, but it couldn't have been too long, or the teacher would have come looking for me, or maybe she wouldn't. Once the throbbing had subsided to a tolerable level, I got myself up and slipped into my classroom. The kids snickered as I tried to walk upright to my desk. My teacher had her back to the class and didn't notice that I came in late. Unless I was being humiliated, I was invisible to everyone.

Chapter 1

I, Karen Lynn Slimick, was born in Alton, Illinois to parents who were born and raised in West Virginia. When I was seven, dad loaded us up with a few belongings into our old car, and we headed for the California bay area. I turned eight years old in the middle of Kansas's cornfields and my dad, Robert, stopped at a small diner where we celebrated my birth with greasy burgers. My siblings and I had expected to see cowboys and movie stars once we entered the golden state, but San Leandro, our new hometown, was pretty much like everywhere else we had lived and we were disappointed. We left behind snow days, dazzling autumn leaves, fireflies, a large extended family and a comfortable midwestern lifestyle.

My brother, Danny, was one year older than me, and my sister Alanna was one year younger. Dad got a job working at a convalescent hospital as a maintenance man, and we were settled into our new life with my mother, Maxine. My mother volunteered at the hospital and assisted the residents.

I developed strong friendships at school and in the neighborhood; I learned about diversity and acceptance. My life experiences in the east were limited to Caucasians, and I don't even remember eating Chinese or Mexican food, let alone seeing other ethnicities. I tried to be polite and not stare at the kids in my new class, but the accents, varying skin shades, and unique faces were fascinating. I am thankful that I was given the opportunity to know and connect with this melting pot of kids. It certainly taught me that we are no different, and we have the same joys, fears, emotions and struggles. We are just different colored crayons in the same big box.

Chapter 2

I experienced my first boy crush shortly after moving into our new home. Michael visited his grandparents, who lived next door to us, almost every weekend. Michael didn't talk much, but would stare at me until I stuck my tongue out at him.

Once afternoon, we heard a quiet knock on our front door. My brother was the first to reach the door and flung it open. He leaned down and picked up a piece of paper and waved it in front of me. "Ewww, it's fer you," he threw back at me with his taunting tone, the tone that only brothers can deliver. When I stepped into the doorway, I saw a large pile of roses, at least three dozen on the porch. "Karrrren, I loves you," my brother read aloud. I snatched the note from him and saw that there was no signature. I suspected it was Michael, but I wasn't sure. I scooped up the roses, stabbing myself several times on the sharp thorns and took them into the kitchen. My mother, wearing a goofy grin, provided several large vases filled with water. I was so glad that my dad wasn't home; he would have teased me to no end.

A short while later, we opened the front door for Michael's grandpa who was visibly upset. My mother stepped in front of us and asked what the problem was. "Did one of your kids cut down my prize roses?" he asked with suppressed anger.

"Why, no sir, I don't believe so, but some roses was left on our porch jest shortly," mother replied. Mr. Grandpa turned around quickly, grabbed Michael by the arm and pulled him to the front. I hadn't seen him behind his grandpa.

"I'm asking again, did you cut down my roses? Don't lie to me boy!"

Michael was looking down at his feet, but then slowly lifted his eyes to meet mine. My eyes locked with his, I was flattered and scared at the same time. Very quietly, in a small whisper, Michael admitted that he had cut the roses. We both knew the wrath of grandpa would soon be upon him, but we had that moment, that shared connection of pronounced love. I smiled at Michael, a sweet, loving grin that I hoped would melt his heart. Suddenly I saw his grandpa smack him up the side of his head.

We all flinched, and my mother asked, "Do ya want yer roses back?"

"No thanks, the damage has been done. You keep them." Then Mr. Grandpa paused, and we saw some of the tension in his face relax, "Please enjoy them. Sorry for bothering you folks, we'll deal with this at home." With that, Mr. Grandpa dragged Michael down the stairs, muttering all the while about his beautiful roses. I watched until they slipped into their front door, waiting to see if Michael would dare to look my way, but he was too busy dodging his grandpa's attempts to make contact with his head.

I went into the kitchen and delicately touched the soft petals of my roses while taking in the lovely scent. I felt such a sense of pride. This young boy risked the wrath of his grandpa to express his love for me. The feelings of being adored were so sweet and profound. This was something new, and I liked it. *Maybe Michael and I would get married when we grew up. We would have a little house of our own with rose bushes surrounding the yard to honor the first moment we shared our love,* I thought.

Suddenly I felt a thump on my head. I spun around to see my brother making a love-struck face. "Ya got that there boy in trouble. Why would he be given' ya flowers?" Danny threw in my face. I lunged at him and just missed punching his shoulder as he jumped back.

"Knock it off ya two, I think it's sweet that Michael likes ya, hon, but he shouldn'ta been cuttin' his grandpa's roses without his pa knowin'." I knew my mother was right, but it made the gesture that much more important.

My little sister confided that evening that she helped Michael with the roses. She appeared to be sad, and I asked her what was wrong. "I tole em that I could be his girlfriend, and he patted my head and said that he loved you." I felt bad for my sister, but I was still flattered that I was the one he chose.

My crush on Michael didn't last very long since Dad announced that we were moving soon to our own home in Dublin. He had a new job, and our tract home was almost built. I wish I could say that I worried about how Michael would handle our separation, but I was nine years old and the excitement of a new home and school filled my every thought. I daydreamed about new friends and how my life would be even better.

In the next few weeks, we packed up what little we had. The residents at the convalescent home where my parents worked were sad to see us leave, and some of our favorite patients gave us small gifts they had made. I had spent many afternoons and weekends in their rooms and in the gardens of this home for the elderly. These people had become like family, and I eventually realized that their tears were justified. We didn't come back and visit the way my parents had promised. It was a long drive and our lives got very busy. Occasionally we would hear through my dad's previous employer that one of our favorite patients had died. Eventually, none of the connections we had made were left.

Chapter 3

We were all settled into our new house, and it was wonderful. Everything was clean, fresh and perfect. The house in San Leandro had charm, but it was old, drafty and dingy. My sister and I would have to share a room, but we could deal with that. After all, we had shared a small room with my brother and an uncle for many months at the old house.

School would start the day after Labor Day. I pleaded with my mother for some new school clothes, but money was very tight due to the house purchase. She insisted that my old clothes would do just fine; they still fit, even if out of style. She explained that she had to focus on buying shoes for all of us kids.

While we finished up shoe shopping at the Big K, my mother browsed the cosmetic department. She gave me an odd sideways look and picked up a box. I was to find out later that this was an at-home permanent. Many women didn't have the money to pay hairdressers, so they used these home products. My mother had done a few perms on the old ladies at the convalescent hospital, and felt qualified to perm my pale blond hair. I don't know what inspired her since I never asked for curly hair.

Sunday afternoon, I was instructed to sit at the kitchen table and preceded to have my first hair experience. The details are fuzzy, except that it took a long time and a lot of mild cursing on my mother's part. Mother was a lady of faith, and if she cursed at all, it was a big deal. I sensed that the perming was not going as well as expected. Once the rods were removed, she rinsed my hair and then dried it. The shock set it. My beautiful, straight blonde hair was now a tight fuzzy pile of cotton. My mother tried several hair products to relax the frizz, but nothing worked and she finally gave up.

"It looks purty dear. It'll calm down in a few days," she said without any conviction.

I went to my room and looked into the mirror. I remember crying as I stared at the chemically burnt mass on my head. I was so angry that my mother did this without asking me. I looked like a big Q-tip.

When I heard the call for dinner, I went to the dining table and slinked into my chair. My brother's reaction said it all. He began howling. My dad managed to get out the words ..."What the heck, Maxine, what did ya ...." before she cut him off with a stern look and said with too much inflection ..

"It looks very sweet on her. Perms is all the rage right now."

Alanna grinned and reached up to pat my head, but I smacked her hand before she could react. I was mortified and ran from the table crying. I flung myself on my bed and wallowed in my shame and anger until I heard a tap on the door and then my dad's voice. "Kin I come in kiddo?" I didn't respond but knew he wasn't leaving. Finally, I gave him permission to enter, and he sat on the edge of my bed and patted my back. "Honey, it don't look so bad. You is such a purty girl, and if anyone kin wear this hairdo, you kin." I rolled over and looked into his lying eyes.

"Daddy, it's horrible. You know the kids is gunna tease me at school."

He hugged me, and said, "Nahhh, the kids'll see what a swell person you is. They won't be carin' bout yer hair. Now git back down to supper. There's a big chunk of yer mother's chocolate cake waitin' for ya."

I lived in a generation that celebrated, consoled, and shared every emotion with food. The draw of chocolate cake was irresistible; especially my mother's because baking was done from scratch when I was a kid, and I knew the rich creaminess of the chocolate frosting would sooth my pain, at least for a while. When I came down to the table, my brother started up again. I took a lot of pleasure when my dad slapped the back of his head. Danny yelped and glared at me. There was a lot of head smacking when I was a kid, but I knew this time was absolutely justified.

After I finished my cake, I hatched a plan since I couldn't start at my new school looking like this. I decided to fake a stomachache right away so that my parents didn't think I was faking on Tuesday morning. I sat in the bathroom until my brother and sister's pounding on the door got my mother's attention. After checking me for a fever and pressing on my stomach, her solution was a healthy dose of X-Lax which is a laxative disguised as chocolate. Figuring in the kick-in time, I was very lucky she gave it to me on Sunday evening since I spend most of Memorial Day on the toilet. I hadn't really thought this faked illness out, and by Tuesday morning, my mother insisted that I was well enough to go to school.

X-Lax was not my friend, we had history. When I was a little kid, my mother put a new bar of X-Lax in the medicine cabinet. She told us not to touch it. Once she was gone, I climbed up and grabbed the bar, which looked very much like a candy bar. I peeled the wrapper back, and it was … deep, rich, dark chocolate. My sister and I split the bar. Kids aren't particular when they think something is a forbidden treat, so the odd taste did not stop us. Several hours later, my mother noticed my sister's multiple trips to the bathroom, and when she found the X-Lax wrapper in the garbage, she freaked out! My sister, of course, ratted me out, and we were taken to the emergency room to get out stomachs pumped. I was scared to death, so I insisted that my brother had eaten his fair share also. I figured he would go first because he was the oldest and he always insisted on going first for everything. If Danny survived, then I knew I would not die. He screamed and swore he didn't eat any, and his version is that he convinced them he was innocent, but my memory is more interesting and we were all taken in and hooked up to the stomach pumping hose. Needless to say, either way, my brother and I were not on good terms for quite some time. To make matters worse, the local paper ran a story about our misfortune, and it was not the type of publicity you want as a kid.

Chapter 4

Our community was growing rapidly, and there were many new housing developments. The city hadn't had enough time or funding to build enough schools for the increasing number of students, so our new school was a cluster of temporary portables. My mother drove us across town and pulled up with all the other parents. My brother climbed out of the car, puffed up his chest and strutted onto the campus. My sister was excited, urging my mother to hurry up so she could complete our enrollment in the office. I slipped out of the car, head down, filled with dread. I knew my father's words were intended to encourage me, but I also knew that he lied, and I would not go unnoticed. This was a time of cool clothes and smooth, straight hair. I felt a sick souring in my stomach and struggled not to throw up. I began to panic that I would add vomit to the embarrassment of old clothes and burnt hair.

After my mother filled out all of the necessary paperwork, we each were assigned a classroom. Danny was going into the sixth grade, I was entering the fifth and Alanna was a third grader. I was in Mrs. Evan's class in Room C-3. I saw some of my new classmates waiting around the entrance of the room, and I cautiously moved up with them, my eyes focused on the ground. Some of the kids were snickering, but I didn't look up to see if it was directed at me.

Once the bell rang, the door opened, and Mrs. Evans greeted us. She was middle-aged, short, and heavy-set with curly gray hair. She didn't leave much of an impression in my memory banks, so I'd say she was tired and stern because you remember the teachers that inspired you. We had assigned seats, and I was near the front; I groaned inside. I wanted to be in the last row, the desk closest to the door. I sat down and lifted my desktop where I found new pencils, paper, a notebook and crayons. The beginning of the school year with everything brand spanking new was a great feeling. I really did love school.

After everyone was seated and the teacher had our attention, she instructed each of us to stand, say our name and tell everyone a little something about ourselves. I must have looked like a deer in a hunter's crosshairs. When it came to my turn, I stood and stared at my desktop as I didn't want to make eye contact with anyone. When I started to speak, the teacher told me I needed to talk louder, and I started again. "Hey yal, my name is Karrrren Slimick (pronounced Slim-Ick), and I jest moved here into our furst new house. I wuz born in Illanoise." The building laughter finally made it into my brain, and I realized they were laughing at me.

I heard the boy next to me say, "She sure talks funny."

"Now class, you need to be respectful, people talk differently all over our country." I knew she was trying to minimize the embarrassment, but I was reeling; I didn't realize my way of speaking would create such a reaction. The way I talked was never an issue at my old school since there were so many different accents. My friends thought I sounded cute, and compared me to Elly May Clampett from the very popular Beverly Hillbillies TV show. I loved the way my family from West Virginia spoke. It was colorful, warm, charming and very soothing to me. I sat down confused and had a very bad feeling that my accent would only add to my fried hairdo that graced my head.

After the introductions were complete, we passed out books and workbooks for our subjects and my desk was filled with the sweet smell of newly printed books. The teacher then announced that we would have a recess break. Generally I loved recess, this gave me time with my friends, to laugh and run, but I purposely moved slowly so that I was the last student out of the classroom. I figured I'd hang out by the classroom door and wait to see if someone nice might approach me. I wasn't a shy kid and certainly could be outgoing and friendly, but I felt odd here, like I had to be careful. I didn't know if it was my own shame or the energy of the students that filled me with apprehension. They seemed to be the poster kids for the California Dream. Most were dressed in new, very cool clothes, great hair and lots of attitude. I grew up with "Yes Sir" and "Yes Maám".

When I came through the door, I saw a group of kids that appeared to be waiting for me, and I smiled thinking that I had been wrong, and they were friendly. Several of the boys pointed and laughed at my hair. My hands immediately moved up to cover and compress the pile. A girl named Janice moved in closer and gave me the once over. "So Karrrren, does everyone in your family talk as weird as you?" This was followed by a group giggle.

"Yeah," I said quietly.

"How did your hair get like that?" another girl asked. I couldn't tell if she meant it as a fair question or a dig. "It looks stupid!" she added as she crossed her arms over her chest while smirking at me. Well, I knew where she was coming from. A yard duty teacher must have noticed the pileup; because she came over and told us to move along. I was relieved as I sat on the wooden planks that served as a walkway between the portables and waited for the bell to ring. I searched the kids' faces to see if I saw anyone with a kind expression looking my way. I knew everyone wouldn't like me, so I just needed to find one or two kids that were friendly. No one made eye contact, and I felt very much alone. Hopefully lunchtime would be better; I would meet some nice kids then. The bell rang, and we filed into the classroom. As I moved toward my desk, I felt someone shove me hard, which caused me to lose my balance. Luckily I caught myself by grabbing onto the desk next to me. The boy sitting at the desk glared at me and whispered, "Don't ever touch my desk again, Freak!" I recoiled not understanding the venom that accompanied the order.

One of our classroom activities would be a new word each day. Unluckily, our word for that day was Bumpkin: a clumsy, awkward fellow. Since most of the class saw me stumble, Bumpkin would briefly be my new nickname.

It soon became lunchtime, and I was getting hungry. I looked forward to the lunches my mother packed because there was always a meaty sandwich, fresh fruit and a homemade snack. The weather was nice, and the kids moved out to a section of picnic tables on the school ground. They staggered lunch times by grades so that everyone could fit and we had two fifth grade classes that had the same lunch break. I walked over to a table that wasn't full and attempted to sit down, but the girls on the bench quickly slid over pushing me off the end. Several other girls sat down at the far end of the bench, which filled it. I wanted to protest, but the challenging expressions of the row of girls intimidated me, so I stood and looked for another table, but they were filling up fast. There was room at the next table, but it was mostly boys, including the boy whose desk I touched, so I knew I would not be welcome there. I noticed another table with mostly kids from the other fifth grade class. They hadn't heard me talk; maybe I could just sit and eat. I sat down and smiled, and several did smile back, but they were quickly involved in a conversation about the cute boy, Steve, in their class. They finished their food quickly and moved on to the playground. I ate slowly and watched the dynamics of the kids. A lot of cliques had already formed. I noticed several kids from my class sitting alone on the wooden walkway and thought I should approach them. Maybe they were feeling left out too, and we could form our own group of friends.

I finished my lunch and saved a chocolate chip cookie to give to Alice. Alice was very tall and lanky with protruding buckteeth and a rash on her bare legs. When I approached and stood in front of her, she ignored me. I awkwardly shifted and cleared my throat. She finally looked up and didn't smile. "Yeah?" she asked.

"Hey, I saw ya sittin' here all bys yerself and thought I'd come over and say hey," I said with as little accent as I could manage. I extended the cookie. "My name is Karrrren."

She glared at me. "I know who you are, and I'm alone because I wanna be."

I wasn't sure what to do next. She didn't accept my cookie, so I stuck it in my pocket. "I jest thought maybe we could be friends."
Alice looked at me without emotion. "If I hang out with you, they will just be meaner." She got up and walked away.

How had this girl decided my fate so quickly? It was only the first day and tomorrow would be better; I always had friends at school, and this year wouldn't be any different. I considered approaching the other girl sitting alone named Lisa, but I saw her pick her nose, inspect her digs and pop it in her mouth; I realized that she would only complicate my situation. Then it hit me; I was Alice's Lisa, and none of us wanted to make our situation worse, so we would not be banding together.

When my mother picked us up after school, I was very quiet. She asked us all how our first day went and if we made friends and if we liked our teachers? All the things a parent asks a kid. My brother and sister had a great day! My sister already had three new friends, and four girls liked my brother, so he said anyway. I couldn't know if he was telling the truth or if it was just his inflated ego. Mother didn't notice that I wasn't sharing and when we got home, I went to my room and stared at my reflection in the mirror. *What happened between fourth and fifth grade that turned me into a kid that everyone hated? I looked the same except for my hair, and I sounded the same,* I thought. The tears began to fill my eyes and spill over. I felt sick to my stomach again and a heavy dread filled my heart and mind. How was I going to go back to school tomorrow and the next day and the next? I lay down on my bed and tried to sleep, but I was unable to escape my reality. The faces of the kids would swirl in my mind as they laughed and snickered at me. I struggled to find a solution to this horrible problem, but nothing came to mind.

My sister popped in, all chatty about her day and her friends. I wrapped my pillow around my head so I wouldn't hear her, but she got up in my face wanting to know what was wrong with me. I screamed at her, "Jest go away. I don't wanna talk to ya or nobody else."

"It's my room too. Ya can't tell me what ta do," she yelled back.

I picked up a hairbrush from the table next to my bed and threw it at her, clipping her leg.

"Mother ... Karrrren threw a hairbrush at me!" she screamed as she ran to tattle.

My mother showed up a few minutes later. "What's goin' on in here? Did ya throw a hairbrush at yer sister?" I didn't answer but began sobbing instead. My mother slid me over and sat on the edge of my bed.

"What's wrong, Hon? Are ya sick?"

"I hate this school, Mother. The kids is so mean!" I had a glimmer of hope that my mother would know how to help.

"Well, it's only the furst day. I'm sure you're jest overreactin'. You gotta put yerself out there if'n you wanna make friends. Jest be nice and smile, and tamarra will be better."

I looked at her encouraging smile and realized that she had no clue. She left me alone, and I stared at the ceiling. I knew God was real, and we could pray to Him and I poured my heart out, asking Him for just one friend. I didn't know if God would be too busy to be bothered with one little kid wanting to be liked, but I hoped He wasn't.

When my sister came back in, she tried to make me feel better, but I didn't want to talk about my day and I ignored her.

Chapter 5

Each morning I'd stand in front of my classroom, fighting tears, willing myself to walk in. My stomach would churn, and I would become nauseous, struggling not to vomit when I stepped into the room. Each day I was greeted with comments, glares and snickers. After some time, my fried perm was finally growing out, but my hair looked worse. I had straight hair at the scalp and then a fluffy ring of fuzz. I tried several times to get my mother to agree to buzz it off like my brother's, but she insisted that it wasn't that bad. "Jest let it grow out some more, Karrrren. Then we kin cut it in a cute pixie."

I wanted to look and sound like everyone else. I was so tired of being treated like a Leper and isolated. Every day was the same. Taunting, name calling, eating alone, recesses alone, occasional acts of aggression which included tripping, shoving, slamming my head in the cabinet doors when I got supplies, and books on desktops shoved into me. The first time it happened, I was unprepared. I was walking to my desk, when suddenly a pile of books slammed into my side. I looked over and saw one of the worst bullies, Bubba, grinning an evil smirk at me. Apparently he waited until I was close and shoved the books as hard as he could. I looked over at the teacher's back and debated whether to tell. I heard a whisper that began to build as other voices joined in. "Snitch! Snitch! Snitch!" I weighed the cost and reluctantly sat in my seat. I knew being quiet wouldn't change anything, but I was convinced that tattling would make it worse.

Being alone in a crowd is so much worse than really being alone. You are physically there, but surrounded by an invisible partition. You can only watch the laughter, interactions and bonding, but it is out of your grasp. The "Lepers", my name for us outsiders, avoided each other and never did unite. Movies endear you to the misfits, they create this very lovable group of talented, eccentric kids that will grow up to be more successful than all the cool kids. This was not my reality of being bullied; we avoided each other like we each had a plague, knowing that things could definitely get worse. Alice had been right … if we happened to be in line next to each other, the comments would start. "The freak show must be in town" or "There's double ugly!" The surrounding kids laughed as if it was the funniest thing they had ever heard. Alice didn't react to the bullying at all. She almost appeared to check out, to go to some place nicer in her head. I would fight tears or the urge to lash back. This was the first school year that I had dealt with bullying, but my guess would be that Alice hadn't been so lucky.

The other two unlucky members of the Leper club were Lisa and Doug. Lisa had short, orange, curly hair. She was covered in freckles, and her build was that of a linebacker. I remember her smile, such a sweet smile, dimples and sparkling green eyes. I didn't see her smile often though. It was only in class when the teacher complimented her on a project she had done well. Doug was tiny, very small for his age with frail arms and legs. His pant legs blew around him, almost as if there were no legs at all. He had thin dark hair that was plastered down with some sort of hair product or oil. Doug always spoke in a whisper, and his skin was pasty pale, almost ghost like. I felt the worst for him since he was obviously very ill. The boys constantly tormented him, and Doug endured their abuse without a word. They would surround him and take turns shoving Doug to the boy on the other side of the circle as he struggled to keep his balance, trying not to collapse when they pushed. Sometimes a teacher would step in, but it appeared that they were blind to the magnitude of harassment and treatment of us Lepers. I guess they figured it was just kids being kids.

I tried on several occasions to tell my parents how bad things were, but they dismissed my concerns with trite comments. "You're bein' too sensitive, ya gotta toughen up!" was my dad's usual advice. I'd also get "Ignore 'em, we love ya." The most insulting was, "Well are ya try'n? Ya gotta be a friend before ya kin have a friend." I can't totally blame my parents for their reaction; they saw me with family and church friends, laughing and acting like a pretty normal kid. I don't think they could even imagine how painful things were at school.

I was involved in our church's youth group. This was a place that I was accepted and felt like everyone else. Luckily, none of the students from school attended our church. The youth pastor and staff were supportive and encouraged us to talk to them about our concerns or problems, and I thought about sharing what was happening at school, but I didn't for two reasons. One, I knew they couldn't do anything about it, but the main reason was, I didn't want to be that kid. I didn't want to acknowledge her, to have them look at me with pity or worse, with recognition that I was treated badly because I truly was a Leper. My self-image was so battered that I needed a place where I could fool everyone and allow them to think I was normal.

Chapter 6

It was February. I'd survived months of belittlement and alienation, and on this day I was in my mad, *"who do they think they are?"* phase. During the school year, I bounced from seething anger to acceptance that I was everything they said I was. I watched the kids swinging at lunch on this particular day and realized that I wanted to swing, I had the right to swing. The school had a procedure so that the swings would be shared. You positioned yourself by a swinger and counted to thirty, and once you reached thirty, they were to get off and give you the swing. The six swings were filled with all boys. I chose one of the center swings, the one that held the least aggressive boy. I stood in front of him, but far enough away so that I didn't get kicked, and began counting. Another boy yelled out "Slimy is counting!" I have to mention here that Slimy and Slimy Slimick were my nicknames at this point. The total focus of the playground was on me, and the SWING INCIDENT had begun.

I didn't know what the boy on the swing had in mind until it was too late. The kick to my pelvis when he leapt from the swing was excruciating, as well as degrading. As I laid on the ground, tucked into a ball, the laughter of the other students went deep into my heart and confirmed that I was hated. Hated for no reason other than I was unique. No one would protect me, no one cared that I was hurt and embarrassed. Without understanding why, I had to accept the truth that there was something very wrong with me. A part of me died that day on the playground, a large piece of my self worth shriveled away.

My dad was a good dad, a kind man, but he didn't know how to handle girl stuff. I was entering the first stages of puberty, and my emotions were all over the place. This included mood swings and crying, he felt, for no reason. Dad decided that humiliating me would cure the water works, and whenever I would display emotions by crying, he would call me "Ol' Cow Eyes".

"Thar she goes again, Ol' Cow Eyes, boohooing and slingin' snot."

I never understood what cow eyes had to do with crying, but I knew the tone. It was ridicule. I didn't want to disappoint my dad, and I made every effort to stop crying and tough out whatever was upsetting me. He made it clear that crying was not acceptable, and it confirmed to everyone that you were weak and pathetic.

That evening at dinner, however, I couldn't hide how upset I was about the brutal assault at the swings. I felt anger and humiliation rising up and then the sobs began. My nose was running, and I was a blubbering mess. My dad, not realizing there was a serious reason for my emotional outburst, began to tease me with "Ol' Cow Eyes" again. The mortification I had already endured on the playground that day was magnified by his taunting, and I shut down. I ran from the table and threw myself on my bed. I could hear my dad reassuring my mom. "She's fine, jest silly girl stuff again. We can't spoil her, she jest has to learn to git through it."

"But she seems so upset," my mother said with concern.

"You goin' in there and babyin' her will jest make it worse. She can't be coddled Maxine, or no tellin' how whiney she can git."

My mother honored his wishes, and I quietly cried myself to sleep.

I was convinced that I couldn't rely on my parents for help. My father saw me as a weak crybaby, and I knew that I could not talk to them about the bullying at school, no matter how bad it got. I knew I would not be able to stop the tears, and that would only get me more humiliation from my parents. This was my defining moment of ultimate isolation, and not even God was helping me. I began to doubt God's love for me. I believed He existed, but He obviously did not care about me.

Chapter 7

Shortly after the swing incident I noticed that one of the very popular girls would watch me. Every time we made eye contact, Tina would look away. It wasn't a look like the other girls gave me. You know that smirky, snotty look. It was curiosity or maybe even sympathy. I knew that I had my place, and she was certainly not accessible to the likes of me. Tina had it all, beautiful blonde hair, adorable clothes, a fancy house and lots of friends. She was the one that everyone tried to sit with, or hang out with. She wasn't mean to me like the other girls, but didn't seem to know I existed either, not until lately. I had my routine, and I had accepted my life. I learned to avoid the avalanches of books and never stuck my head into the cabinets so that the doors could be slammed on me. I couldn't avoid the comments, looks and shoves, but at least I wasn't getting physically hurt.

I had held out hope that when my hair was cut into a stylish pixie, I wore more current clothes, and minimized my accent, that I might fit in. It didn't work that way; I was labeled Slimy, and that was that. It didn't matter now what I did. I think part of my survival was the fact that I wouldn't be attending this school next year. The permanent school in our neighborhood would be open for next fall. Since this school was so far from my house, I assumed I would be a city away from these kids. I knew there was an end to my prison term so I could survive anything for a little while longer. I focused on enduring one day at a time.

On a Friday, I was waiting with my brother and sister for our ride at our designated spot. Mother had instructed us to walk to this corner to be picked up each day so she could avoid the congestion in front of the school. My brother and I were horsing around with each other when I heard my name.

"Karen." I turned, and there stood Tina. I must have looked shocked because she quickly said "I just want to talk to you for a sec."

I stepped away from my brother, who of course followed, but I shoved him away before he could embarrass me. Normally he would have shoved me back and tried to flirt with Tina but my expression of *"I will kill you"* must have been intense.

I stood there looking at her without a clue about what she wanted. Why would she want to talk to me? "Ahhh, I just want to say that I feel really bad how the kids are treating you. They are so mean," She paused. I'm still quiet, waiting. "I really like how you draw." I did love to draw, and I put a lot of effort into school assignments and art projects. My drawings were posted quite often on the classroom bulletin board. "I like to draw too," she continued.

"Oh, me too," I exclaimed. *How stupid, of course she knows that,* I thought.

"I was wondering ... if you weren't doing nothin' ... if you wanted to come over to my house this weekend. We could do a sleep over if you want," Tina explained.

I almost fell to the ground. So many thoughts slammed through my brain. Was this a trick? Did my mother call her mom? I finally managed a quiet "Why?" I wanted to trust this girl but every experience I had at this school screamed "No, don't, it's a trap!"

"I think you're nice, and I think we could be friends."

What? Us friends? You never talk to me at school. This doesn't make any sense. Trap! Trap! But what uttered through my lips was "Sure! If my mother says its okay."

"Great, here's my phone number." Tina handed me a piece of paper with the right number of digits. Could this be for real? I looked around to see if there were kids hiding, watching, and waiting for Tina to humiliate me when I believed what she was saying, but there was nowhere for any one to hide. My head was filled with disbelief, warnings, and hope. This could change my life if she was being honest. If this popular girl were my friend, everyone would have to be nice to me. I allowed myself to feel excited about the possibility of change!

"Oh, Karen?"

"Yeah," I said with a grin.

"You can't tell anyone. This has to be a secret."

My soaring heart plummeted, and I watched in shock as she walked away.

On the drive home, my mind was racing. I was excited, angry, mortified, thrilled and confused. I couldn't agree to be a secret, but I didn't want to be friendless either. I was hurt, and I was flattered. What was I going to do? "Mother, do we have any plans for this weekend?"

"No, jest church on Sunday. Why?"

"That girl asked me to come to her house fer a sleepover."

My brother jumped in, "Tina asked ya over fer the weekend? Man, she is so cute. Ya gotta put in a good word fer me."

"I'm not gittin' ya girlfriends," I explained with a pained look.

Then he puffed up, "I don't need yer help. I can git her or any other girl on my own."

"You're too young fer girlfriends Danny," my mother teased. "That's great dear, I need to talk to her mom furst before I kin say yes. Ya don't sound too happy 'bout it. Do ya even wanna go?"

I had to make a decision. Maybe we would be a secret at first. Once we were real friends, she wouldn't keep me a secret then. "Yeah, I wanna go."

Later that day my mother dropped me off at Tina's house. They lived in the rolling hills west of the Dublin valley. Our house was nice, but hers was huge; two stories, a pool and a great view of the valley. She took me up to her room, and it was every girl's dream. Pink and lacey, she had her own record player and a small TV. She showed me all of her photo albums from when she was a baby till then. Tina was amazing; she excelled in dance, gymnastics and soccer.

I didn't want to ruin our time by asking her why I was there, and why I must be a secret, so I just enjoyed being a girl doing girl stuff. We danced in her room with the music blasting. We ran in the hills behind her house., and I got to going so fast down the hill that I lost my balance and rolled head over heels till I reached the bottom. I was okay except for some bruises and scrapes. We lay in the grass and laughed and laughed. Tina said that she'd never seen anyone roll down a hill that fast before. Our time was filled with all the things girls do, and it was wonderful.

That evening in the dark we shared secrets and stories about our lives and families. It was getting late, and I thought Tina had fallen asleep since she had been quiet for some time. "Karen, why do you think the kids at school pick on you so much?"

"I don't know. I had lots of friends at my ole school," I answered.

"You did look kinda weird when school started, and I hate to say it, but you talk funny. Not so much now, but at first."

"I know. I'm guess'n I was jest too different fer the kids here. My ole school had all kinds of kids. We had African kids, Mexican kids and Chinese kids, and everyone talked and looked different. Here … everyone is white and fancy."

"I'm not fancy."

"Well kinda, ya have a real big house and lots of clothes."

Tina was quiet again, and I finally got the nerve to ask her. "Tina, if ya wanna be my friend, why does it have ta be a secret?"

Tina didn't answer for a long time, and again I thought she had gone to sleep. Eventually, I heard her take a deep breath. "If the kids know I like you, I'm afraid that they will be mean to me too."

"But maybe that wouldn't be how it was at all, maybe they would be nice to me too."

"I don't think so. They hate you, and they won't stop teasing you. Me being your friend won't change nothin'."

I lay there awake thinking about what Tina said. She was asleep now; I could hear her deep breathing. I had to decide what I wanted to do. If I told everyone that we were friends, she would hate me and probably join in with the torturing; after calling me a liar of course. I could ignore her and just not be her secret friend, but the problem was, I really liked her. Tina was funny, crazy and sweet, and our day together was so much fun. As much as I resented being a secret, I would be the only one losing out if I didn't go along. Finally, I fell asleep after accepting my decision.

The rest of the fifth grade was spent surviving each school day, and wonderful weekends with my family and Tina. It seemed that we were at one or the other's house every weekend, but she didn't speak to me at school. Tina didn't join in with the others when they taunted and humiliated me, but she never stood up for me either. She just uncomfortably watched the show from a distance.

While we were friends, school was never discussed after that first night in her room. I didn't want to pressure her and maybe lose her, so I accepted the secret friendship for what it was and for what Tina could offer. A part of me understood why, but most of me just felt sad and unworthy. I knew I was settling for crumbs, but I wasn't going to give up what little I had.

Tina abruptly moved away the first week of summer and we never spoke again. I have mixed feelings about Tina. We shared so much in those last few months of fifth grade, but I always wondered what would have happened if she had been honest about our friendship. Would it have altered the next four years of my life?

Chapter 8

A new family had moved into our neighborhood in June, and they had two sons younger than me, Greg and Larry, but they were fun and hung out with my sister and I. Their dad brought home a baby fox he found abandoned at his work. Buster was adorable, and we would play with him as if he were a puppy or kitten. We didn't realize that foxes were carnivores until we heard our huge duck, a pet from Easter, flapping his wings and squawking. Buster had grabbed our duck, Ducky, by his long neck and was trying to drag him into the bushes. The duck weighed much more than the fox, and there was a real battle going on. Ducky was beating the fox with his wings, but the fox was inching their way into the cover of shrubbery. It wasn't funny for our duck, but we laughed as we pried Buster's mouth from around Ducky's neck. Several days later the boys showed up crying and heartbroken. Their fox had gotten out during the night, and someone shot this beautiful creature and left it on their front porch. Whoever killed Buster knew that he was a family pet.

My family was doing very well financially, and my dad surprised us with a horse. Rabbits was an odd looking horse, long ears and a brat; he'd try to bite. We learned how to ride, groom and shovel huge piles of poop over the summer. I certainly did not enjoy the smell and the flies that come with a stable, but I loved the rush of flying on the back of a horse. Dad added six more horses over the next few years.

My summer was filled with new adventures, but I was excited for school to begin in the fall. I knew that everything would be different in the sixth grade, back to normal. I would have friends at my new school and Slimy would no longer exist. She was dead forever!

Chapter 9

When the first day of school arrived, I was up early, primping and trying on everything in my closet. I had selected my outfit the day before from my new, cute school clothes but changed my mind about twenty times. I ended up wearing the same outfit I had originally laid out.

We lived close enough to our new school to walk, and when it was time to leave, the excitement of a fresh start was pulsing through me. As my sister and I neared the school, I saw kids climbing out of cars, riding up on bikes and walking as we were. I felt the excitement building. We were almost to the front steps when I heard a loud voice boom out … "Hey, it's Slimy Slimick!" and then the laughter. I turned to the source and saw a group of students from my fifth grade class. My confusion blocked my understanding for a few moments; the worst offenders from fifth grade were in front of me. Students that I didn't know began to laugh also. The blood drained from my face. I was not free from my torment, it had followed me here.

I quickly moved to the lists of classroom assignments. There was my name, in a room with many of the kids from fifth grade. A sickening dread filled me. I was trapped, and there was nowhere to run. How could I have been so stupid to think that they would all still be at the portables? But how could I have known? I wasn't friends with any of them, so I had no idea they lived in surrounding neighborhoods and would be attending my new school.

The bell rang, and I entered my first class. Seating appeared to be first come, so I found a desk in the back corner. As my former classmates filed in, I saw the recognition on their faces. *Yes, it is I, Slimy Slimick*, I thought. I almost wanted to stand up and curtsey. Then the whispering started, and the new students were informed of my lowly status. Everyone was looking over at me. Some of the new students looked confused and others had that look of *"Thank God, they already have a Leper chosen!"*

I saw my fellow Lepers enter the room last, Alice and Doug. I then understood the resignation I had seen in Alice's eyes last year. This was a cruel joke that just didn't end. No, I was not going to accept that this year would be a repeat of last year. There were a lot of students that didn't know Slimy, and I could certainly find a friend or two in this much larger school.

It was lunchtime and my class headed out to the cafeteria, which doubled as the school gym. When I walked in, I saw the same cliques grabbing tables, and I didn't consider sitting with them. I saw a table with a few kids that looked as beaten down as I felt. Doug was there, and the rest were new faces from different classes. I moved toward the table and felt someone move up behind me, close. I turned and was face to face with Bubba. "That's it Slimy, go sit with the other losers." The group of kids that were coming up to sit at the nearby table overheard and began laughing.

"Slimy, now that's funny," one of the new faces said loudly, which prompted more laughter from the group of onlookers. I didn't respond to the boy and moved to the cafeteria exit. I wasn't giving Bubba the satisfaction of telling me where to sit. A big boy in a yellow vest stopped me.

"No food outside," he said.

I dropped my lunch into the large garbage can by the door. Once I was outside, I slid my backside down a tetherball pole and waited for lunch to be over. The kids began to wander out as they finished eating. Two girls from my class that I didn't know walked toward me and stood at my feet. "Move, we wanna play," one of the girls said rudely.

I got up and asked if I could play too. Their names were Diane and Cindy. "No thanks," said Diane with indifference. I started to insist that I could play too, but stepped back when Cindy snarled, "We don't want you here, no one wants you here Slimy."

"What did I ever do to you?" I asked.

Cindy lifted the ball and punched it, aiming at my head. I ducked and backed away. I was back in my nightmare, and I couldn't wake up.

I found a patch of grass under a tree and sat. I couldn't cry, I knew that would be like chumming the ocean for sharks.

A very popular show on TV, McHale's Navy, had a character named Captain Wallace Binghamton. He was the butt of most jokes on the program and had the nickname Leadbottom. The kids decided that this was the perfect nickname for me when they got bored with Slimy. As a developing young girl, I assumed my butt was too big if they called me Leadbottom. This mean nickname began a fixation on my body image and my weight. I was convinced that these kids could correctly decide what I should look like, and they decided I was too fat. The bullies had done their worst, and I could pretend I didn't believe their insults, but deep in my heart I knew they couldn't all be wrong. My battle for self-worth was in full force, and I was losing. I began to hate my body and tried to hide the curves that were part of the natural process of growing up. I didn't see the real me in the mirror, I saw fat Leadbottom.

Chapter 10

There were a few kids that would talk to me and let me sit at their table without humiliation, but even they kept a safe distance. I wasn't invited to parties, sleepovers or just to hang out. It's like everyone knew the pecking order and stuck with it. I kept a very low profile and stayed as invisible as possible. I watched Alice and Doug trying to do the same, but we were trapped entertainment.

It really was only a few that were aggressive about the abuse. The problem was the majority that stood by and watched, or laughed, or joined in once the show got started. I think that most of them were smart enough to know that they wouldn't be the targets as long as the Lepers were available. They certainly knew that Leper was contagious and weren't going to get close enough to catch it.

Jessie, a new boy transferred to our school. He was a big boy with a strong build. Jessie appeared to be timid and stayed to himself, watching the other boys on the playground. I didn't realize at the time that he was focused on Doug and the torment he was enduring each day. Jessie had only been attending our school a couple of days when a profound event played out.

The bullies had Doug encircled as usual, pushing on him, knocking his books to the ground. Doug was an avid fan of the James Bond 007 books, and the boys took delight in throwing his books onto the school roof. Suddenly, Jessie stood up from the bench where he had been watching. He walked over to the group of boys and began pulling them off of Doug by their shirt collars. Everyone on the playground froze and watched the drama unfold.

Once Jessie was next to Doug, he growled, "This is my new best friend. If you wanna mess with him, you will be going through me." The bullying boys stood there, humiliated. Several looked as though they might challenge Jessie, but obviously thought better of it. The boys slinked away and regrouped at the far side of the playground.

Jessie helped Doug pick up his books, and they left the area. We rarely saw Doug without Jessie, but when we did, the group of bullies were on him.

I admired Jessie with every part of me. Obviously it helped that he was a big boy, but it still took a lot of courage and compassion to put himself out there for someone else. I so badly wanted to approach Jessie, to let him know how much I liked him, but the fear of how the rest of the kids would react prevented me from following my heart. I also worried that Jessie would panic, that he would think by befriending Doug he had opened the gateway for the rest of us Lepers to swarm in. He might abandon Doug, so I adored Jessie from afar, so wishing that I had someone that would stand up for me.

Jessie and Doug remained close friends until Doug's death at nineteen. I never did know what was wrong with him, but it brings me great comfort to know that Doug had a dear friend and protector throughout the rest of his short life.

Chapter 11

One evening my mother and dad sat us down to explain that dad's job wasn't providing enough income, and he had agreed to manage a friend's apartment complex for a few months to get us by. We would be moving in two weeks. My siblings were not happy about the move since they had friends and a life in Dublin, but I was thrilled! I looked at this move as an opportunity to take a break from my nightmare. We would be living in Hayward, a good distance from my schoolmates, so no surprises this time.

We had a heated pool, and that was great fun except for the twin boys who lived next to the pool area. It didn't matter what I was doing, if they caught me anywhere near the pool, I was dragged to the edge and pushed in. They thought this was hysterical! I fought with everything I had, but ended up sputtering in the deep end every time.

After one of these ambushes, I marched into the apartment, wet and angry. My dad looked up from the TV and told me to dry off, I was leaving a wet trail on the carpet. After putting on some dry clothes, I plopped down on the couch, letting a long sigh slip out. My dad looked over and realized I was upset. "What's wrong kiddo?" he asked. I explained about the twins and how frustrated I was to be pushed in over and over.

"Ya want me to talk to their folks?"

I had thought about that but realized that it would probably make things worse. I didn't want the kids thinking I was a snitch. Other than the unwanted plunges in the pool, I was just like the rest of the kids here at the complex and actually had friends. The twins would make it their business to make my life miserable if I ratted them out.

"No Dad, I guess I'll just deal with it."

"What do ya do when they grab ya?" he asked.

"I fight back, I try to kick them, and I scream in their ears."

"Here's some advice. Next time … don't fight. When they git ya to the edge of the pool, jump in."

"Are you serious? Why would I do that? They shouldn't get to do what they want, and I shouldn't help them."

"I know it doesn't make sense, but trust me, jest try what I'm telling ya. They want to feel powerful, and if you don't fight, it won't be fun for them, and they will find someone else. Hon, its just water." Dad went back to the TV, and I knew this life lesson was over.

The next day, I had to go throw the clothes into the dryers for my mother. The laundry room was right next to the pool, so I peeked around the corner to see if the twins were in the vicinity. I didn't hear or see them, so I ran quickly but quietly to the laundry room, and put the clothes in the dryers. I checked the pool area again and they were in the water, wrestling with each other, trying to hold the other one down until someone gave up. I could have avoided the pool by going around the entire complex, but decided to risk it. They would have to see me, get out of the pool and grab me before I could get through the far gate. I would run fast!

I was half way to the gate when I heard, "Tim, get her." I ran faster, but when I reached the gate, Tim had caught up to me and grabbed me by my arm. Ted was quickly on my other side, helping Tim drag me to the water. While they were laughing and making rude comments, I looked into their dripping faces and decided to trust my dad, and I stopped fighting. They pulled me to the edge of the pool, and before they could push, I jumped in pulling them in with me. When they popped up, sputtering, the look of surprise on their faces was priceless. I got out of the pool without saying a word and went home.

Several days later, they grabbed me again. I willingly walked to the pool edge, and I jumped in.

"Well this sucks," Tim said. "You're no fun."

That was the last time they tried to throw me into the pool. I would watch them drag screaming kids to the water and laugh while they tossed them in. I still haven't sorted the whole life lesson out. Is it picking your battles? Letting the strong rule? Fighting back is foolish? Don't feed into the drama? This could be applied in so many ways, but I just know that it worked and I was thankful for that.

I didn't try to help the other kids that were now being thrown in; I was just glad the twins were not focused on me. This was a perfect example of why the kids at school did not stick up for me when they saw me being bullied. Our natural instinct is for self-preservation and avoidance.

Our time at the apartments was over, and I was the only one not happy to be leaving. Summer was almost over, and my personal torture would begin again.

Chapter 12

There was a new energy around me when school started that fall, a lot of whispering and judgmental looks from the kids, which could only mean they knew something important about me that I didn't know. Another student, Grace pulled me aside one day, and she looked embarrassed.

"Is it true what they are saying about you?" she asked.

"That depends, what are *they* saying?"

"You moved away to have a baby," Grace whispered. "Is it true?"

I felt my face getting hot, and my stomach began to churn. I hadn't even kissed a boy and they had me pregnant. "No, it ain't true," I threw at her. She walked over to a group of girls and relayed my response. I could tell no one was buying it. I ran to the far end of the field and let the tears roll down my cheeks because I knew this was only going to get worse.

Puberty brought on a whole new dimension to the ritual of torment. Not only was I a Leper and disgusting, but now the rumors said I was doing nasty things with all kinds of boys. The thing I couldn't figure out was, who were they talking about? The boys would act like they were dying if they bumped into me, but I'm messing around with everyone?

I was all-alone in this new phase of the nightmare. I was too embarrassed to tell my parents about these disgusting rumors, and I believed they couldn't do anything anyway. If they showed up at school, it would have made things so much worse.

The teachers were blind to the bullying and the plight of the Lepers. I do not remember a teacher ever asking me if I was okay or if I needed to talk. I do not think that they had a clue what was going on. I had to figure out how to survive on my own.

Chapter 13

I was shocked when I found out that a boy named Billy actually liked me. It was complicated because I had a big crush on Billy's half-brother, Ben. It was Ben who told me that his brother liked me, and insisted that I would like him back. I struggled to have a response, but I couldn't find the words. I didn't dislike Billy, but he was like a lump of bread dough, pale, spongy and no personality. Ben, on the other hand, had an adorable face, muscles, sun streaked blonde hair and was very aggressive to the point of mean. I found him irresistible and had spent many hours foolishly daydreaming about a romance. Ben informed me that he and Billy would be at my house on Saturday. I didn't argue because Ben said he was coming too.

As Ben walked away, I got the nerve to ask, "Why does he like me?"

"No one else is going to like him, and you have boobs," he threw over his shoulder.

Saturday afternoon was finally here. Ben and Billy showed up on my porch, and my mother was polite but cool. This was the first time a boy had come to see me, let alone two. We awkwardly sat in silence at the kitchen table while we picked at a snack I had set out. After only five minutes, Ben jumped up and announced that he had to leave for another girl's house, and I was crushed. Ben then leaned down and whispered,

"You be nice to him Slimy, or you'll deal with me."

After several attempts to start a conversation with Billy, I realized it was hopeless. He just sat and picked at the rubber on his tennis shoes. I explained that my family was going to visit relatives, and he had to leave. This was a lie, but I just couldn't sit there in total silence any longer. I walked Billy to the door and said goodbye. As he headed to the sidewalk, he turned around and paused. I waited, curious to hear what he would say.

"Ben says you're gonna be my girlfriend, so you have to sit with me at lunch."

I was mad, not all the spunk had been bullied out of me yet. "I am so sorry Billy, but I am not your girlfriend. You are a nice boy, but I don't like you." I marched back into the house. *How dare Ben decide who I would like. He had his nerve.* I remembered the adoration of Michael and the roses. That is what I wanted and deserved, and I longed for the feeling of being cherished. I would not settle for what Ben had in store for me.

That next Monday, if I looked in Ben's direction, he glared at me and brought his finger across his throat. Apparently, this was to warn me that he was going to chop off my head. I knew he wouldn't really, but I didn't know what he would do. Billy just stared right through me with no expression. I was very nervous and waited for Ben to make his move. Lunch came and went, and then PE was over. These were the two prime opportunities to take me out; maybe I was in the clear.

The final bell rang, and as I pushed through the halls, I felt a hand on the back of my neck, squeezing. I looked behind me, and it was Ben. He brought his mouth down to my ear and said, "I warned you," and then he was gone.

I wasn't sure what to do, I was worried, but I didn't think telling anyone would help. He hadn't done anything, not yet and didn't say what he would do. Maybe he was just trying to scare me.

I left the school grounds to walk home. I got about four blocks from the school and suddenly felt a painful hit on my head. I turned and saw a rock on the sidewalk. Before I understood what was happening; I felt another rock hit my chest. I looked up to see Ben and Billy. Ben had a handful of rocks and was preparing to throw another one. I turned to run, and as I fled, I felt the impact of the rocks that made contact with my body and saw more rocks hitting the sidewalk around me. I ran up to a small group of kids and pushed ahead of them. When I looked back, Ben and Billy were gone. Once I got home, I checked to see if I was bleeding, but other than some red welts, I was fine.

I asked my mom if she could pick me up after school because I did not want to walk home. "That's silly Karen, we're only twelve blocks from the school, you can walk. I already have to drive to the school everyday to pick up your sister after tutoring."

My heart sank, I considered telling her about the boys with the rocks, but I was afraid she would go to the school and make things much worse. I didn't know what Ben would do if I told on him, and I didn't want to find out. I kept quiet and dreaded what tomorrow afternoon would bring. I prayed that he had gotten his revenge and would leave me alone.

Ben must have told the other boys about hitting me with rocks, because they were very focused on me throughout the next day. They would bump into me in the halls, make snide remarks and several tossed paper wads at me in class when the teacher's back was to us. Billy wouldn't look at me. I couldn't tell if he was mad at me or ashamed, but Ben's glare was easy to read, a hateful stare that hurt me to the heart. I foolishly adored this boy.

After the last class, I started the long walk home. When I entered the strike zone, I felt a large rock hit me on the butt, just below my backpack. I didn't bother to look back, but started to run. I heard a single set of footsteps running behind me. When I glanced over my shoulder, I saw Ben gaining on me. Billy was nowhere to be seen. I turned forward again and pushed myself to run even faster as the rocks pelted my legs and the back of my head. Suddenly, I heard Ben yelp and then scream, "Let me go!"

Once I got a safe distance down the street, I stopped so that I could look at the commotion behind me. A man had hold of Ben's arm and was clearly upset with him.

"What is wrong with you Ben? Throwing rocks at a girl? I think your father will be very interested to hear about this!" the man said with a threatening tone.

"No, no, don't tell my dad. I won't do it again. Please don't tell my dad," Ben pleaded.

I felt a huge wave of gratitude for this man who must have known Ben and his family. I didn't wait to see what happened next, I ran the rest of the way home.

I didn't have any more issues with Ben throwing rocks or getting physical, but if looks could kill, I would be dead many times over.

Chapter 14

Seventh grade melted into the eighth grade. I say melted because it was the same faces, same experiences day after day. Some days I was invisible and others not. On my invisible days, I was thankful that no one bothered with me. The visible days were less and less often as the school year moved along and I did everything possible to keep it that way. I avoided answering questions in class, I didn't sign up for activities, and I never opened a conversation with anyone. I sometimes pretended that I was a ghost, haunting the school. I kept my face down and didn't make eye contact unless I had to. A rude remark or nasty glare would bring me back from my pretend world, and the painful reality would still be there.

I was delighted to discover a glimmer of light in this dark place. There was a new Science/Art teacher that was young, handsome and fascinating. He would let us come into his classroom during lunch break to draw and listen to music. What used to be a painful time of exclusion had become a haven for me. Mr. Humphrey introduced us to new, raw performers from the Haight-Ashbury area. I remember one in particular … Porpoise Mouth. I can't say I really liked them, but I felt very cool listening to this strange new music that my parents would hate. I purchased a pair of hip hugger, bell-bottomed, paisley, corduroy pants with my babysitting money, and Mr. Humphrey loved those pants. I would have worn them every day if I hadn't known it would make me look like a dork.

I was tolerated by a group of kids that appreciated art, music and Mr. Humphrey's influence. This teacher acknowledged my talent as an artist, and I earned a new respect for myself. Stepping into this classroom was a portal into a whole different world. I was Karen, the artist, and I had this passionate teacher to thank for that confirmation.

Sadly, I became Slimy again when I left the safety of the classroom. The kids from the art group didn't join in on the bullying, but they didn't defend me either. While I was in "Humphrey World", I had a taste of being normal and I cherished every moment of it.

Several times I started to tell Mr. Humphrey about the bullying, but I couldn't. It would bring the darkness into this wonderful world, and I didn't want to ruin it. I didn't want him to look at me with pity, so I kept my pain to myself once again.

Chapter 15

My brother, sister and I flew back east for several weeks at Christmas to visit family. My parents were staying in California, so it was going to be quite the adventure without them ruining all the fun. When we got into Illinois, it was freezing. We left San Francisco at 50 degrees, and St. Louis airport had to be 50 degrees below zero. We were not prepared. My cousin Betsy was horrified that we were wearing socks with our tennis shoes. The style there was no socks, but I explained that she could be nuts and freeze her toes off, but I was not losing mine to frostbite!

On Wednesday, my sister and I went to school with Betsy; her winter break started a week later than ours. When we arrived at her English class, the teacher gave us attitude when my cousin asked if we could sit in on the class.

"Why aren't you in school? I don't know of any schools around here that are out for Christmas break yet," he challenged.

"We're not from around here," I explained. "We are visiting from California."

Now you have to understand that this was December 1966. California was considered a very cool place if you lived in Illinois and were under the age of thirty. Adults over thirty thought we were all lunatics and hippies.

"Oh California, I visited San Francisco several years ago. It was fabulous. Of course, you can visit our classroom, we are honored to have you here," he said with genuine admiration.

I was flattered, and I felt very important, but that was nothing compared to Friday. I decided to go back to school with Betsy on her last day before holiday break and you would think Marilyn Monroe was in the building. When we walked down the hall, the kids parted like the sea when the Jews escaped from Egypt. After being tormented for my hillbilly accent, I was being complimented for my Californian accent. The kids said that I sounded like I was from England. Odd, I know, but very cool at the time. They stared and gawked at the girl from California. I was a celebrity, and the attention was delicious.

At lunchtime, my cousin took me to a hamburger joint across the street and announced that she was going out with her boyfriend, Matt, that night and I needed to select a guy so we could double date. I looked at her in amazement. *Me pick out a date?* I thought, *Betsy is crazy.* "No one is going to agree to go out with me!" I declared.

"You are a pretty celebrity from California who can have anyone she wants," Betsy insisted. "Seriously, look around, who do you want to go out with? I will tell Matt to set it up," she assured me. I froze up and just stared at her. She truly did not see the real me, the Leper. "If you don't choose someone, I will," she said as she began to search the room with her eyes.

"Okay, okay," I said. She had truly lost her mind, and I was going to put an end to this delusion quickly. I looked around the room and saw a gorgeous blonde with tan skin, bright blue eyes and a big white smile. "Him," I said as I pointed at the boy and I waited for her to laugh hysterically.

"Okay, I don't know him, he just moved here, but when Matt comes, I'll have him talk to him."

I looked at her with a frantic expression; she was really serious about getting me a date. I suddenly felt horrified; this boy would take one look at me and go into fits of uncontrollable laughter. I couldn't bear the humiliation, not here, not when I was feeling so special.

"No, Betsy, let me pick someone else. He's not going to agree to go out with me," I insisted.

"Nope, that's the one you want, that's the one you get."

Before I could convince her, Matt walked in and gave Betsy a big kiss and squeeze. She whispered in his ear, and he grinned.

"I'm on it," he said as he winked at me.

Matt was adorable, a freshman with a car, the perfect boyfriend. I had met him at the house when we first arrived in Illinois. I watched Matt walk over to the beautiful boy, and I wanted to disappear. I tried to slip away from Betsy, but she grabbed my arm.

"You're not going anywhere, he will say yes," she whispered.

Matt was speaking, and the boy looked over at me. He had no expression while Matt talked to him. The beautiful boy said something to Matt in response. Next thing I know, Matt is coming over to us and the blonde dreamboat was leaving.

"He said no, right? I told you he wouldn't want to go out with me," I said to Betsy as my cheeks got redder and redder. I was silly to allow myself to feel special. The attention I had gotten as a Californian had lulled me into a false sense of acceptance, but I was still Slimy, nothing could change that!

Matt grabbed Betsy's hamburger and took a big bite. Through meat, cheese and ketchup I heard him say, "We pick him up at seven."

"What's his name?" Betsy asked.

"Andy I think. I've never met him before, he's a lowly eighth grader."

Betsy pretended to slap Matt for his teasing insult while I sat there speechless. Betsy looked at me with a confident grin and said, "I told ya he would say yes." I could only nod as my stomach began to do flip-flops.

I went through alternating waves of emotions while I waited for seven o'clock to arrive. I felt disbelief, excitement, dread, hope, embarrassment, suicidal, thankful but mostly scared. I had never been on a date before. I knew my parents would not approve, so we told my uncle that the three of us were going to get a pizza, and we just didn't mention Andy. It wasn't really a lie; no one asked if anyone else was going with us.

I began to fantasize; maybe he would hold my hand; I might even get my first kiss. Andy was so good looking, too good looking to ever be interested in me if we were home, but I counted on my advantage, I was from California. I saw how the kids looked at me in awe when they had found out, and that's why Andy agreed to the date. I just needed to relax and dazzle this midwestern boy while I remembered that I was a celebrity in hip hugger, bell-bottomed, paisley, corduroy pants.

At six forty-five, Matt was honking his car horn out front. "Betsy, that boy needs ta be more respectful and at least come up to the door," my aunt scolded.

"Okay ma," she said as she grabbed my hand, and we ran out to the car.

Betsy got in the front seat with Matt, and I slid into the backseat, and we were off.

"Do you know where Andy lives?" I asked Matt.

"Yep, let's go get your dream boy," Matt teased.

Betsy smacked his arm playfully. "Don't, she's nervous enough without you making it worse," she said in my defense. I saw the devilish flicker in his eyes that were framed in the rear view mirror and I could tell he wanted to tease me further, but he honored Betsy and winked instead.

We picked up stunning Andy, and when he climbed into the back seat, he didn't sit on his side as I expected, he slid all the way over until he was up against me, and put his arm over my shoulder while I was freaking out. I had no idea what to do, so I sat there, stiff as a board. I kept reminding myself that I was in control. I was a California celebrity, and I didn't have to say anything; he would be so thrilled just to be with me.

"Andy, when did ya move here," Matt asked.

"My dad got transferred here three weeks ago," Andy supplied. "We lived in L.A. before here."

Oh no! My heart sank, he is from Los Angeles? Seriously, out of all the boys in that restaurant I picked the only Californian? It all made sense now, the tan and sun bleached blonde hair. No one from Illinois had a tan in December, tanning booths were not invented yet. This was my lousy luck, this guy was the celebrity and even I was impressed that he was from L.A.

"What part of California are you from?" Andy asked me.

"Central, close to the bay area."

"That's cool, never been up that far. Hear the beaches aren't that great past Big Sur so never bothered to head farther north to surf."

A surfer, I picked a surfer, how much cooler can this guy get? He is probably related to the Beach Boys. I can't impress this guy, and he will realize that I am a Leper girl before the evening is over. There will not be a first kiss, I thought. I wanted to shrink into myself.

He leaned over and whispered, "Go along."

"So, you got those big sharks along the coast up there too?" he asked. "The ones that are eatin' people?"

"Oh yeah, got another guy just before we left. Ate every bit of him.

They say his wife got it all on her movie camera," I added.

"Really, the sharks are big enough to eat a man?" Betsy asked in amazement.

"Yep, more and more of them all the time. So bad you have to swim with a group and take harpoon guns," Andy insisted.

"But that's not the worst of it," I said. "The sharks are changing so they can breathe air. One woman was half eaten when a shark crawled up into her beach house," I said fighting the giggles.

"I think I heard about that," Matt contributed. "It's revolution or something weird like that."

"Yeah, and they got a new problem off of San Diego beaches. The Piranha have escaped from the Amazon, and they have bunches of them that swim in packs along the coast. You stick your toes in the water, and they eat the meat off of your legs up to your knees before you can even pull them out," Andy threw in when it was his turn. "The news stations are getting paid off to not report them, cuz they need the tourists to keep coming with their money."

"Oh man, that's so not cool!" Matt exclaimed.

When I started laughing, Andy tried to cover my mouth.

"You guys are such big fat liars," Betsy said as we pulled up to the pizza parlor. Betsy and Matt jumped out and waited for us to join them. Luckily they were both grinning and appreciated the joke.

"Give us a few minutes, we'll be right in," Andy said as he held me back by my arm.

They knowingly grinned at each other and walked in to order a pizza.

I was freaking out, wondering why Andy wanted to stay in the car. He closed his eyes and brought his face close to mine. Here it comes, here it comes, my first kiss, and then I felt his lips on mine, soft and tender. It was wonderful. He kissed me again, firmer this time, pulling me closer to him. I felt butterflies in my stomach, and it was magical. My first kiss was everything I thought it would be.

Then suddenly, I felt something wet pushing against my lips. His tongue, he was trying to stick his tongue in my mouth. I pushed him away and wiped his spit off of my lips. "That is disgusting," I said, "You're not putting your tongue in my mouth." I had no knowledge or experience with French kissing, so I just thought he was weird. Andy pulled away from me, and he was mad. He slid over to his side of the seat, crossed his arms across his chest, and he wouldn't even look at me.

"I like kissing you, but why do you want to put your tongue in my mouth?" I naively asked.

"It's called French kissing, everyone does it. But you're just a little girl and you are stupid," he said with venom.

I tried to apologize because I really wanted to keep kissing him, but he wouldn't speak to me. He just sat against the door, staring out through the steamed windows.

Matt came out to announce the pizza was ready, and we silently followed him inside. Andy totally ignored us while he stuffed pizza into his face. On our trip to the restroom, I explained what happed to Betsy. She laughed and said, "He's an idiot, and we'll head out soon."

Needless to say, it was a quiet drive home. We dropped off Andy, and when Matt took off, he squealed the tires.

"What a jerk he was," Matt supplied. "He didn't even offer to chip in on the pizza."

"Yeah, a real jerk," I agreed. *But what a good kisser*, I thought to myself.

When we got back to the house, Betsy took a shower while I wallowed in the pain from the horrible evening. My first date fantasy that I had created years ago was now shattered. How dare I think I deserved any better. I was found out for who I truly was and Andy was proof of that. I was a stupid Leper.

When Betsy returned to her room, she asked me, "What are the chances you would pick out a guy from California? He's got to be the only one in town," she said giggling.

"I know, right? I was already to impress one of your farm boys," I said sadly. "Maybe the tan and sun bleached hair should have been a clue."

Betsy looked into my tearing eyes with such concern and then we both suddenly burst out laughing. Tears continued to run down my cheeks, but it was from mixed emotions; disappointment and the irony of my stupid luck. I felt the heaviness in my heart flow out of my "Ol Cow Eyes" and I didn't care.

After we calmed down, I asked Betsy if she and Matt French kissed. "Not talkin' about this any more, especially not with someone who thinks French kissing is gross," she said with a teasing grin.

I threw a pillow at her and hit her smack in the face, and Betsy stuck her tongue out at me and wiggled it for emphasis.

When we were settled in, Betsy asked, "Was he a good kisser, when he kept his tongue in his own mouth?"

"Oh yeah, that part was nice. He was definitely a good kisser!"

"So the whole date wasn't a bust. You did get your first kiss you know."

"Yes, I did. I need to thank Matt for that. Don't think I'll be talking to Andy any time soon to thank him."

We both began to giggle, so loudly that my uncle banged on the wall and told us to "Pipe Down."

I drifted off to sleep with visions of Andy, perched on a surfboard in the middle of shark-infested water; sun bleached blonde hair blowing in the wind while his tongue waved at me.

I have to say, being famous while in Illinois was really memorable, especially for a girl who was a Leper in reality. I dreaded my return home but, I was thankful that I got to pretend to be special for a little while.

Chapter 16

When I was invited to Carol's slumber party, I was shocked and thrilled. Maybe things were changing; maybe I could be a normal kid. I picked out the coolest outfit I owned, insisted that my mom buy me new pajamas, and I found the perfect birthday gift and card. I had heard all about slumber parties, doing hair, nails, snacks and staying up most of the night. This was going to be the best party ever.

My mother dropped me off and told me to remember to brush my teeth. *Yeah, right,* I thought! *I'll be eating snacks throughout the night, when would I brush my teeth?* I went up to the door struggling to carry my sleeping bag, pillow, gift and overnight bag. After ringing the bell, I realized I was holding my breath. I breathed in deeply and wore a grin from ear to ear. Carol opened the door and just glared at me without speaking.

"Hi, happy birthday," I said.

She reached out her hands and looked at me annoyed when I didn't respond. She looked at the gift under my arm and emphasized her waiting hands again.

"Oh, the present, here, this is for you." I said as she snatched away the carefully wrapped box.

"You can throw your stuff over there," she finally said as she pointed to the items on the living room floor, and left me standing on the porch as she walked back into the family room filled with music and squealing girls.

I added my belongings to the big pile in the living room that was adjacent to the entryway and followed the voices. Once I stepped into the room, I was staring into the shocked faces of my class's elite. Eight of the most popular girls were dumbfounded at my presence. I sat down on a chair in the corner, and tried to relax. I hadn't really thought about how I would be accepted or why I was invited; I was just so thrilled to go to my first slumber party. Carol's mom was setting up for another game before the pizza was to be served. She smiled at me and assigned me as the first member of one of the teams. I was relieved that the girls weren't choosing teams; I didn't want to be embarrassed by being the last one chosen again.

My heart had been hopeful that this would be a wonderful night, and I was invited because Carol really did like me, but my gut was beginning to read the truth of the situation.

The games were fun, and the hot pizza was gooey and delicious. The girls were civil but cool when Carol's mother was close by, but when she left the room, they were overtly hostile to me. I was confused, I had been invited. After all the games were played, the evening turned to talking, primping and trying on each other's clothes. When I offered to let Nora try on my precious hip hugger, bell-bottomed, paisley, corduroy pants, she looked at them with a sneer.

"They're kinda cool, but way too big to fit me, or probably anyone else here."

I felt my face turning red. I sneaked a peek at my bottom in the reflection of the sliding glass door. I did not have a large butt. Nora's butt and hips were much bigger than mine. It was very clear that no one was going to include me in this activity of clothes sharing, especially not after Nora's loud comment. No one would want to risk fitting into my pants or having them be too tight. Even worse would be if their clothes were too big on me. No one was going to risk being larger than fat Leadbottom. I watched as they laughed and posed and shared. I was afraid that I might cry, and I wasn't going to let them witness my weakness. I decided to go into the bathroom and cried as I changed into my pajamas.

I returned to the group and walked up behind Carol and Nora who were loudly discussing me.

"Why did you invite Slimy? That's just weird," Nora sniped.

"I didn't, my mom did. She knows her mom and said that we needed to be neighborly. I didn't think Karen would come, not when she knows that none of us like her," Carol complained.

When they realized I was behind them, they moved over to the other girls and began laughing hysterically at the conversation in progress. They looked at me long enough to give me a nasty dismissal and then resumed their laughing.

I had a decision to make. I could get my stuff and walk out; show them that I didn't need them or their party; that I had my pride, and they couldn't humiliate me. Instead, I sat down and sadly watched the party that was beyond my reach and wished so badly that I could be them.

I struggled to stay awake until the last two girls finally stopped gossiping and fell asleep. I was afraid of what they might do to me if I fell asleep before them. I could see them playing a prank that would humiliate me even further.

I woke early the next morning, called my mom and packed up to leave. Carol's mom had to tell Carol to thank me for coming and for my gift. She did, but it was empty and obviously painful for her. I was so embarrassed, but not by their treatment. I was mortified that I stayed once I knew why I was invited. I wanted to be a strong person that wasn't going to take any garbage off of anyone, but I was weak, pathetic and needy. No wonder no one wanted me around, I didn't want to be around me either. I was an absolute loser.

The rest of the eighth grade moved slowly. Some days my invisibility didn't work, and I was like the toy that was forgotten and found again under the sofa. There was a renewed interest and energy, which subjected me to public mortification and insults.

When things were calm for a while, I would be hopeful and think I might be an equal, but I was quickly reminded of who I was. I look back, and I am amazed at my ongoing optimism that things could improve for me. I suppose that was really my only option for self-preservation. To give up is to be defeated and I couldn't let them win.

My thread of hope was high school. Most of these kids would be going to the same school, but I knew that we would be freshman, and all of us would be on the lowest end of the food chain. There would also be a blend of many junior high schools; which meant new possibilities for friends.

I did find acceptance during these difficult junior high years with my cousins, my church's youth group and my siblings. Our youth group was active, and I enjoyed many wonderful experiences with these loving kids. When I was part of this group, I felt a warm wash of love come over me, and it gave me strength to deal with my days at school. My sister and I fought a lot, but we spent many hours talking, pretending and dreaming aloud. She was an important part of my survival.

My face says it all!

Danny, Karen, Maxine
and Alanna

Chapter 17

High school provided a large supply of kids that did not know me from junior high and I was able to make friends. Some of my haters would do their best to humiliate me when they saw me on campus, but I was able to lay low most of the time. I was excelling in my art classes, and loved the expression it provided.

Sadly, whenever I began to feel confident, someone from the past would spot me, and I'd hear "Hey, Slimy" screamed at me from across the schoolyard. I would just pretend I didn't hear them, hoping that no one new would connect me to the name. I hesitated to participate in school activities including dances; I felt like I was always waiting to be ambushed. It was so difficult to trust that I could be just another kid; the years of humiliation changed how I saw myself, and that was such a sad outcome.

My church youth group was going on a sledding trip that winter. We were bringing toboggans, sleds and saucers, and everyone was excited about the fun in the snow. My first ride was down a steep hill with many large moguls. The toboggan was supposed to hold four, but we squeezed on five. We hit the moguls at a very high speed, bounced quite high, and then slammed back down on the hard, icy surface after each bounce. The boy behind me fell off and slid the rest of the way down the slope on his belly and face. I grabbed the girl in front of me and held on for dear life. We crashed at the bottom of the slope when we hit a large wall of icy snow. I was lying on my back, taking inventory. Everything seemed to move and wiggle the way it should, so I attempted to get up. Suddenly a man ran up, yelling, "Don't move, you need to stay still." I was confused but followed his orders.

Several adult men lifted me enough to lay me on the toboggan, and I was carried to the parking lot. I stared into frantic faces, but no one was saying anything. The adults decided to place me in the back of a station wagon and raced me, my sister and one of the chaperoning adults to the nearest hospital. I scared Alanna with my cries every time we made a sharp turn on the curvy roads. After doctors, nurses, x-rays and questions, I waited in a small examining room with no idea what was going on.

"Your father is on his way dear. He should be here soon," the chaperone informed me with a sniffle.

"My dad? Why?" I began to feel alarmed.

"Well dear, he's taking you to a larger hospital. You have crushed vertebra in your back," she said sadly.

I had no idea what that meant, and we waited in silence until she started to cry.

"I've never known anyone who broke their back before," she blubbered.

"Who broke their back?" I asked.

"Well, you dear, you broke your back," she said softly.

"What? My back is broken?" I understood that! I felt the panic beginning to build. *What does this mean? Can I walk, will I be in a wheelchair, where is my dad?* I began to freak out at this point. The woman tried to console me, but she had been the bearer of the bad news, and her delivery sucked. I needed my dad.

I didn't have to wait long. He called a friend who owned a small plane, and they flew up to the mountain town where we were. I saw the fear in his eyes and knew that this was very serious. He held me the best he could without lifting me up, and I cried while we waited to be released from the hospital. There was no mention of Ole' Cow Eyes.

Once I was loaded into the small plane, we flew back to an airport by my hometown. An ambulance took me to our local hospital, and I was admitted. There were more x-rays, more doctors, and some embarrassing questions.

"Hello dear, how are you feeling?" one of the doctors asked when he entered my room on the third day of my hospital stay.

"Fine." I said.

"Excellent," the doctor said. After a long pause, he asked, "I need to know if you have passed gas since the accident?"

"Huhh?" I said

"You know, passed gas?" he asked again with an animated facial expression.

I didn't know what he meant and gave him a confused stare.

"Ahhhh," another long pause, "Have you farted?" he said while turning bright red.

"Nooo, it wasn't me," I said mortified.

"It's okay Hon, I want you to fart. It's a good thing if you fart." The doctor was visibly embarrassed.

I didn't know what to say. I had farted but didn't want to tell this strange man about it.

"It means that your system is working correctly. If you aren't far…, passing gas, there could be something wrong," the doctor explained.

"I guess I have, maybe a couple of times," I reluctantly admitted.

"That's great," he responded with a huge smile. "Just what I wanted to hear." He left the room quickly. I'm not sure who was more embarrassed in our exchange about "Passing Gas".

I stayed in the hospital for a week. The good news was that I could walk, but I would have to be very careful for some time and allow my spine to recover and heal. I didn't really understand all the doctor's explanations, just that I wouldn't be in a wheel chair and could go home. They were preparing something for me that would help with the healing process.

When my parents arrived at the hospital to take me home, some therapists came into my room carrying a large metal cage. They were discussing this metal cage with my parents, and I didn't fully understand what they were saying until I heard …

"She will have to wear this brace for six months. It needs to be put on while she is lying down and taken off when she is lying down. We don't want her to stand up without it."

What? Six months, I have to wear this huge, ugly metal cage for six months? It's not fair, I won't do it! I screamed in my head. The tears rolled down my face. My heart ached at the thought of going to school and wearing this horrible brace. Everyone would see it. I was inconsolable.

Once home, and in my brace, I stood before the mirror. I couldn't hide this portable cell under my clothes. It was too big and bulky. It would have to be worn in plain sight where everyone could see it.

When Alanna came into the room, I thought she was going to laugh and make fun of me, but she quietly sat on her bed and said, "It's not so bad. I'm just glad you're okay. I was so scared Karen, I didn't think you would be able to walk again." I saw true affection in her eyes, and I did feel a little better. She never teased me about the brace.

My mom drove me to school my first day back. I was so thankful that I didn't have to ride the bus, but my relief was only brief. I would be riding the bus home and every day after that. She went into the office with me and explained my limitations to the vice principal. I would be removed from physical education for the rest of the school year, and I was given a study hall class with seniors instead.

My mother gave me a hug and told me that it would all be just fine, no need to worry. Right mother, that's how it's always been, "just fine". She had the luxury to leave, I didn't.

The time in the office made me late for class, so the campus and halls were empty. I just had to make my grand entrance in English. I opened the door, took a deep breath and stepped in. The teacher and every student stared with their mouths gaping open. Mrs. Nelson finally spoke, "Hello dear, we are so glad to have you back. Please take your seat, we are on chapter twelve." I struggled to fit myself and "The Cage" into the desk opening. The teacher realized my dilemma and motioned to a chair and table to the side of the room. The humiliation became more and more suffocating as she stopped the class to accommodate "The Cage". The teacher moved some display items to make a workspace for me. Some of the kids had looks of empathy, but others snickered at my awkwardness. I couldn't wait to be thrown into the general population of my school.

Things were not as bad as I expected. As the shock of my brace wore off, there were three reactions. First was concern and consideration. Friends I had made before the accident were kind and supportive. I began to feel comfortable with them, and the brace was not so significant. The second reaction was indifference. Once the students stared a few times, they really had no interest in the brace or me. The third came from the haters from junior high. When I ran into them, every effort was made to embarrass me, and I think I was getting tougher skin because I found them annoying rather than injuring, but sometimes they could still manage to pierce my heart with their comments. "That cage makes her look even fatter!" or "Could you look any more pathetic Slimy?"

The year moved by quicker than I expected. The six months of "The Cage" was finally at it's end, and we were at my last doctor's appointment. The doctor briefly examined me and removed the brace.

"Well, my dear, you appear to be doing very well. You will no longer need to wear this."

Hallelujah, hallelujah I sang in my head.

We thanked the doctor and left. I felt wonderful. It was surprising how heavy and bulky the brace actually was. It was like anything else … after you've carried it around for a while, you get used to it. I almost felt light enough to float if I jumped up.

Wedding Day, 1972
My sister Alanna and me, the bride.

Chapter 18

In the middle of my sophomore year, we moved to a town called Livermore. This clean break was as if a switch had been flipped, and I was a normal kid again. I had friends, boyfriends, and no one knew about the Leper girl. You would think that all would be good with the world, but I knew who I really was. Slimy was now in my head and my heart. When I looked into a mirror that is who I saw. I pretended that everything was okay, but I had a secret, and I was scared that someone would find out.

I graduated from Livermore High School in 1971, and attended Heald Business College in the fall. I was engaged to my high school sweetheart and should have been very happy. But a suffocating sadness covered me. Simply escaping Slimy did not heal my broken self-image.

I didn't understand yet that I had to learn how to love Karen; I had to see my value and beauty before I would believe that others could love me. To get there, I had to go through a process that included sharing the pain with people I trusted, counseling and my relationship with God.

It was a journey of discovering who I truly was, not who some mean spirited children decided who I should be. With support and love, I found the real Karen. She is funny, intelligent, creative, compassionate, and a warrior. Yes, a warrior that is brave enough to challenge abuse.

Never too old to instigate!

The Significance of the Dandelion ...

When I began writing, I thought, I am so old. Why am I starting this now? Then I remembered the dandelion. It lives it's life as a flower, fresh, bright white and strong. When it's ready to die, it dries up and looks similar to the gray head of an old soul. The wind then takes the seeds of this dying flower and spreads them throughout the area.

I loved the idea that even though I'm old by most standards, I can still spread my ideas through my stories. Planting seeds that I hope will grow and become considerations for the reader. You will see the dandelion on every book I write, it reminds me that I am not too old to INSTIGATE!

Instigate ... to cause (something) to happen or begin.

From the Author:

Thank you for reading my story, and I hope that I have touched your heart. I have shared the painful details of my childhood to encourage children who are bullied to ask for help, to be honest about the abuse. I hope to help parents, teachers and students understand what a bullied child looks like, acts like, and endures; the terrible isolation they suffer and the damage that can injure their heart and spirit for years to come.

As an adult, I can see my childhood from a different perspective. I should have been honest with my family and the school staff, and I shouldn't have settled for humiliating compromises. But when you are a child in the middle of the nightmare, it is all about survival. When you believe that you are alone, it is easy to become defeated and accept someone else's lies as your truth.

The trials of the bullying were painful and harsh, but I took away some positive outcomes. My experiences taught me that I am strong and that I can overcome adversity! I have faced many difficulties in my lifetime with the understanding that I can endure and succeed. The abuse instilled in me the desire to help others who are hurting, and I am blessed to be married to a man who feels the same way. My husband and I have expanded our family by adopting two wonderful daughters. We have opened our home to multiple single moms who needed a place to regroup and get back on their feet, and my empathy for children inspired me to become a foster parent, volunteer at shelters, youth groups and community projects that benefit children.

The bullying was a powerful, negative energy that I allowed to shape me into who they thought I was … not who I was destined to be. When I look back over my life, I realize that the years of torment were only a small piece of my life's puzzle, a puzzle that also contains joy, friends, incredible memories, accomplishments, respect and love. It is important to know that your life will contain many puzzle pieces and eventually you will see the whole picture, a life made from many events and choices … your own unique puzzle.

My life has been blessed with so much joy. I am married to an incredible man who would chop down roses for me, and I own my own graphic art business, which pays me to create. I have a wonderful family that love and support me, and I am a writer that entertains the minds and hearts of readers. My life is so much better than the sad, heartbroken Slimy ever dreamed it could be. I am thankful that I found my own truth and did not settle for less.

Bullying
Who Are You?

WHAT IS YOUR ROLE IN
THE BULLYING EPIDEMIC?

Tina: You see the abuse but are afraid
          to step up and make a difference.

Ben: You find your worth by
          hurting others.

Jessie: You are willing to take a stand
          against bullying and abuse.

or

Karen: You are fighting to survive.

There are solutions to end bullying; there are ways to stop the harmful behaviors that are so prevalent in our schools. The following information is intended to inform and encourage students, parents and teachers to come together and protect the hurting kids. I pray that each of you will join me in bringing dignity to all children.

Bullying

Do not Believe the Lies

WHAT CAN I DO IF I AM BULLIED?

1 Tell your parents and be honest about what is happening at school. They need to know the truth.
2 Tell your teacher or an adult at school that you trust. Silence does not resolve the problem.
3 Ask your friends to help, to back you up when bullies try to intimidate you.
4 Do your best to ignore a bully if they are only using words. They want you to react and this allows them to feel strong. It is still important to report the verbal abuse to your teacher and parents.
5 Avoid bullies on campus when you can.
6 If someone is physically hurting you, do not ignore them, report the assault immediately to adults (teachers and parents).
7 Get involved in activities such as sports, dance, gymnastics, or youth groups through churches in your community as a way to build friendships away from school.
8 Try to remember that your school years are a small piece of your life's puzzle and is not your forever.
9 Value the positive people and experiences in your life, we foolishly allow bad experiences to be more powerful than the good.
10 Consider how you treat others, and be honest with yourself if you need to be more respectful to fellow students.
11 Do not believe the bullies' lies. They do not have the right to decide who you are.

THE "PURPLE NOSE" THEORY

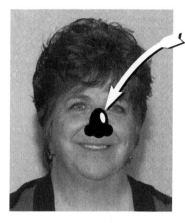

This would so be purple if I could print in color.

If someone said to you ... "You have the biggest, ugliest purple nose I've ever seen." What would you think? Would you believe them and try to hide your nose? Or would you think they were silly and making up lies? Could they convince you that you really have a purple nose, and that you should feel bad about yourself?

You know for sure that you do not have a purple nose, and there is power in the truth. This untrue insult would not hurt your heart. You would just think they are foolish.

If someone tells you that you are ugly, stupid or worthless, this is another big lie, just like saying you have a purple nose. Try to remember what makes you ... YOU. Think about the qualities and talents you have. Maybe you are a wonderful artist, musician, thoughtful helper, loyal friend or have other incredible qualities. There is something special about each of us. If you forget who you really are, you might believe the bully's lies, and that can be very painful. If you remember the truth about yourself, YOU DO NOT HAVE A PURPLE NOSE, YOU ARE NOT STUPID, UGLY or WORTHLESS, you can stop some of the hurt feelings the bully wants you to feel.

WHAT WE ACCEPT AS TRUTH ...
WILL DWELL IN OUR HEART AND SPIRIT.

Do Not Believe the Lies!

Bullying

You Can Make a Difference!

WHAT CAN I DO IF SOMEONE IS BEING BULLIED? – I'M JUST A KID

1. Tell an adult if you see someone bullied.
2. Help the student move away from the bully without putting yourself in harm's way.
3. Be a friend to kids who are bullied and excluded by the other students. Include them in school and non-school activities.
4. Be a good example for other students, and treat everyone with respect.
5. Do not encourage a bully; do not laugh at their bad behavior or their mean comments to another child. If you do, you are telling the bully that it is okay to be hurtful.
6. Get involved in the Anti-Bullying Program in your school, or start one if none exist.

Bullying

Who Has the Power?

People think bullies are in charge, but who really has the power? The few bullies or the student body who stand by and watch without doing anything? Any one can become the target for a bully at any time, so no one can ignore the problem. As a united group, you can make a difference and help children that are being hurt every day at your school. If students join together in Anti-Bullying Programs, you will be saying loudly ...

"We will not remain silent and
allow ourselves to be victims.
We are united and we will protect each other."

You must decide what you will do to end bullying, because if you do nothing, that is a decision based on apathy. You have chosen to allow bullying to continue in your school, and in your community. If you care about others and can feel their pain, then you have empathy. You are the type of person who can help change the lives of children who are suffering.

APATHY: Lack of interest or concern, especially regarding matters of general importance; indifference to others.

EMPATHY: The power of understanding and imaginatively entering into another person's feelings.

Bullying

Why Do You?

WHAT CAN I DO IF I AM A BULLY?

1 Admit to yourself and trusted adults that you are a bully.
2 Think about why you bully and how it makes you feel better about yourself. We do not keep doing something unless there is a benefit for us.
3 Many children that are bullies are bullied themselves. Ask for help if family, siblings, or any one else is abusing you.
4 Remember that any respect and status you think you have earned is based on fear. The kids who support your behavior see you as hurtful and they do not want to have you turn on them. Your actions do not endear you to others.
5 Try to put yourself in your victim's place and acknowledge the heartache you are creating. How would you feel if kids treated you the way you are treating others?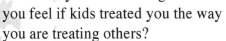
6 If you cannot stop the behavior on your own, get help from adults and counselors.

Bullying

Is My Child a Victim?

INDICATORS FOR A BULLIED CHILD

1 If there isn't any interaction with other classmates away from school, no party invitations, no phone calls or friends visiting, this could be an indication of isolation by their peers.
2 Child's hesitancy to ride the bus, walk to school or attend after school activities.
3 Child tries to avoid school (unusual frequency of illness or physical discomfort complaints).
4 Damaged or missing clothing and/or belongings.
5 Unexplained physical marks or injuries.
6 Dramatic changes in your child's behavior: depression, agitation, or anxiousness.
7 Loss of confidence or your child begins to display low self-esteem or self-loathing behaviors or dialogue.
8 Self-inflicted harm.

SUPPORTIVE ACTIONS

1 Be aware of how your child is experiencing school on a social level. Ask them about their friends, what they do at lunch and recesses. Get specific; ask for their friends' names and activities they play. Kids can be vague and provide answers that do not reveal the truth regarding bullying or isolation. "Everything is fine" should not end your attempt to communicate with your child.

2 If you suspect a problem, press your child gently to talk. Reinforce that they are loved, and they can trust you. Children may be reluctant to talk about bullying due to shame or fear.

3 If your child reveals that there is bullying, do not trivialize what is happening. They may withdraw and stop discussing important situations with you.

4 DO NOT call parents of abusing children or behave aggressively with the school staff. Calmly notify the school that there is an issue and work with the staff to solve the problem. They have experience with bullying and should have procedures in place. Fear about your reaction could be one of the reasons your child may not be honest about being bullied.

5 Encourage your child to get involved in school activities and non-school activities (church youth groups, boy or girl scouts, sports, music, etc). This can provide opportunities to make healthy friendships.

6 Switching schools may be a solution for extreme bullying, especially if the abuse follows them from grade to grade. Sometimes a child needs a fresh start, but give the school the opportunity to address the problem first. Allow your child to experience the possibility of resolved conflict before you remove them. It can be empowering for them. Physical abuse may limit your options so that you can ensure your child's safety.

7 Be objective about how your child is interacting with their classmates. Children can create some of their own isolation issues due to how they are treating others.

8 Be aware of cyber bullying. This was not an issue when I was a child but is now a real threat to our kids. I recommend that you have access to your children's online social accounts and monitor them for predators or bullying activity.

All children will encounter teasing, fickle friends and isolated mistreatment. We cannot protect children from everything negative and we can't demand punishment every time a child's feelings are hurt. This creates a tricky balance for parents and teachers.

My deep concern is for targeted children who are bullied on a regular basis, who struggle with embarrassment and isolation to the degree that it affects their self-image. We want children to be self-sufficient and able to handle the common conflicts that life presents, but it is imperative to know what they are dealing with, and if they need us to step in and shield them from true abuse.

Disclaimer:
The events in this story began fifty years ago, and it is difficult to remember every detail precisely. The dialogue is written to accurately represent the emotions and intent of the event. I have changed the names of the characters (except for my immediate family) to provide privacy for the innocent, as well as the guilty. The interpretations of behaviors are mine, from my perspective as a bullied child.

Suggestions for resolutions are based on online research, as well as my experience as a bullied child and as a parent. I am not presenting myself as a trained psychologist providing professional advice.

The Purple Nose Theory was my explanation for my own children who sometimes encountered teasing at school. You have my permission to share this story about truth with your own children. If it didn't solve the problem in the moment, it at least made my children smile.

If you would like to contact me,
please email me at karnpriester@gmail.com.

Dedications

I would like to dedicate this book to the people who love me.
Your gifts of encouragement and support strengthened me during
my journey to healing. Because of you, I was able to find
my joy and passion for life.

I also want to dedicate this book to Jessie. I have not used your real
name, but if you read this, you will know who you are. You have no
idea how your compassion for Doug touched my heart. I have often
wondered where you are and if you continued to be a person of
great strength and character.

I also want to mention my secret friend, Tina. I have so many fond
memories of our time together. The circumstances were not ideal,
but I love you for what you were able to give me during a very
dark time in my life.

My sister Alanna, you were a good sister and I will always
consider you my bestest friend.

Jenn, your birth triggered such a
profound desire to feel again,
to love again, to make myself
available for a sweet creature with
a precious smile. You were the
very bright light at the end of my
dark tunnel.

Donald, my love, you finished my
healing with your patience and
adoring love. You were the "one"
and I am sorry that it took so long
for us to find each other.

Don proposed to me, onstage, at a PWP dance.

Made in the USA
Charleston, SC
05 March 2014